FRANCIS FRITH'S

OXFORDSHIRE PHOTOGRAPHIC MEMORIES

THE FRANCIS FRITH COLLECTION

www.francisfrith.com

Francis Frith's

OXFORDSHIRE

PHOTOGRAPHIC MEMORIES

Francis Frith's
OXFORDSHIRE

◆

Nick Channer

First published in hardback in the United Kingdom in 2000 by
The Francis Frith Collection®

ISBN 1-85937-076-4

Paperback edition published in 2001
ISBN 1-85937-430-1

Reprinted in paperback 2006

British Library Cataloguing in Publication Data

Oxfordshire Photographic Memories
Nick Channer
ISBN 1-85937-430-1

The Francis Frith Collection
Frith's Barn, Teffont,
Salisbury, Wiltshire SP3 5QP
Tel: +44 (0) 1722 716 376
Email: info@francisfrith.co.uk
www.francisfrith.com

Printed and bound in Great Britain

Front Cover: OXFORD, *High Street 1922* 71989t

The colour-tinting is for illustrative purposes only, and is not intended to be historically accurate

Aerial photographs reproduced under licence from Simmons Aerofilms Limited.
Historical Ordnance Survey maps reproduced under licence from Homecheck.co.uk

Every attempt has been made to contact copyright holders of illustrative material.
We will be happy to give full acknowledgement in future editions for any items not credited.
Any information should be directed to The Francis Frith Collection.

AS WITH ANY HISTORICAL DATABASE THE FRITH ARCHIVE IS CONSTANTLY BEING CORRECTED AND
IMPROVED AND THE PUBLISHERS WOULD WELCOME INFORMATION ON OMISSIONS OR INACCURACIES

CONTENTS

FRANCIS FRITH: *Victorian Pioneer*

FRANCIS FRITH, Victorian founder of the world-famous photographic archive, was a complex and multitudinous man. A devout Quaker and a highly successful Victorian businessman, he was both philosophic by nature and pioneering in outlook.

By 1855 Francis Frith had already established a wholesale grocery business in Liverpool, and sold it for the astonishing sum of £200,000, which is the equivalent today of over £15,000,000. Now a very rich man, he was able to indulge his passion for travel. As a child he had pored over travel books written by early explorers, and his fancy and imagination had been stirred by family holidays to the sublime mountain regions of Wales and Scotland. 'What a land of spirit-stirring and enriching scenes and places!' he had written. He was to return to these scenes of grandeur in later years to 'recapture the thousands of vivid and tender memories', but with a different purpose. Now in his thirties, and captivated by the new science of photography, Frith set out on a series of pioneering journeys to the Nile regions that occupied him from 1856 until 1860.

INTRIGUE AND ADVENTURE

He took with him on his travels a specially-designed wicker carriage that acted as both dark-room and sleeping chamber. These far-flung journeys were packed with intrigue and adventure. In his life story, written when he was sixty-three, Frith tells of being held captive by bandits, and of fighting 'an awful midnight battle to the very point of surrender with a deadly pack of hungry, wild dogs'. Sporting flowing Arab costume, Frith arrived at Akaba by camel sixty years before Lawrence, where he encountered 'desert princes and rival sheikhs, blazing with jewel-hilted swords'.

During these extraordinary adventures he was assiduously exploring the desert regions bordering the Nile and patiently recording the antiquities and peoples with his camera. He was the first photographer to venture beyond the sixth cataract. Africa was still the mysterious 'Dark Continent', and Stanley and Livingstone's historic meeting was a decade into the future. The conditions for picture taking confound belief. He laboured for hours in his wicker dark-room in the sweltering heat of the desert, while the volatile chemicals fizzed dangerously in their trays. Often he was forced to work in remote tombs and caves where conditions were cooler. Back in London he exhibited his photographs and was 'rapturously cheered' by members of the Royal Society. His reputation as a photographer was made overnight. An eminent modern historian has likened their impact on the population of the time to that on our own generation of the first photographs taken on the surface of the moon.

VENTURE OF A LIFE-TIME

Characteristically, Frith quickly spotted the opportunity to create a new business as a specialist publisher of photographs. He lived in an era of immense and sometimes violent change. For the poor in the early part of Victoria's reign work was a drudge and the hours long, and people had precious little

free time to enjoy themselves. Most had no transport other than a cart or gig at their disposal, and had not travelled far beyond the boundaries of their own town or village. However, by the 1870s, the railways had threaded their way across the country, and Bank Holidays and half-day Saturdays had been made obligatory by Act of Parliament. All of a sudden the ordinary working man and his family were able to enjoy days out and see a little more of the world.

With characteristic business acumen, Francis Frith foresaw that these new tourists would enjoy having souvenirs to commemorate their days out. In 1860 he married Mary Ann Rosling and set out with the intention of photographing every city, town and village in Britain. For the next thirty years he travelled the country by train and by pony and trap, producing fine photographs of seaside resorts and beauty spots that were keenly bought by millions of Victorians. These prints were painstakingly pasted into family albums and pored over during the dark nights of winter, rekindling precious memories of summer excursions.

THE RISE OF FRITH & CO

Frith's studio was soon supplying retail shops all over the country. To meet the demand he gathered about him a small team of photographers, and published the work of independent artist-photographers of the calibre of Roger Fenton and Francis Bedford. In order to gain some understanding of the scale of Frith's business one only has to look at the catalogue issued by Frith & Co in 1886: it runs to some 670 pages, listing not

only many thousands of views of the British Isles but also many photographs of most European countries, and China, Japan, the USA and Canada – note the sample page shown above from the hand-written *Frith & Co* ledgers detailing pictures taken. By 1890 Frith had created the greatest specialist photographic publishing company in the world, with over 2,000 outlets – more than the combined number that Boots and WH Smith have today! The picture on the right shows the *Frith & Co* display board at Ingleton in the Yorkshire Dales (left of window). Beautifully constructed with a mahogany frame and gilt inserts, it could display up to a dozen local scenes.

POSTCARD BONANZA

The ever-popular holiday postcard we know today took many years to develop. In 1870 the Post Office issued the first plain cards, with a pre-printed stamp on one face. In 1894 they allowed other publishers' cards to be sent through the mail with an attached adhesive halfpenny stamp. Demand grew rapidly, and in 1895 a new size of postcard was permitted called the court card, but there was little room for illustration. In 1899, a year after Frith's death, a new card measuring 5.5 x 3.5 inches became the standard format, but it was not until 1902 that the divided back came into being, with address and message on one face and a full-size illustration on the other. *Frith & Co* were in the vanguard of postcard development, and Frith's sons Eustace and Cyril continued their father's monumental task, expanding the number of views offered to the public and recording more and more places in Britain, as the coasts and countryside were opened up to mass travel.

Francis Frith died in 1898 at his villa in Cannes, his great project still growing. The archive he created continued in business for another seventy years. By 1970 it contained over a third of a million pictures of 7,000 cities, towns and villages. The massive photographic record Frith has left to us stands as a living monument to a special and very remarkable man.

Frith's Archive: *A Unique Legacy*

FRANCIS FRITH'S legacy to us today is of immense significance and value, for the magnificent archive of evocative photographs he created provides a unique record of change in 7,000 cities, towns and villages throughout Britain over a century and more. Frith and his fellow studio photographers revisited locations many times down the years to update their views, compiling for us an enthralling and colourful pageant of British life and character.

We tend to think of Frith's sepia views of Britain as nostalgic, for most of us use them to conjure up memories of places in our own lives with which we have family associations. It often makes us forget that to Francis Frith they were records of daily life as it was actually being lived in the cities, towns and villages of his day. The Victorian age was one of great and often bewildering change for ordinary people, and though the pictures evoke an impression of slower times, life was as busy and hectic as it is today.

We are fortunate that Frith was a photographer of the people, dedicated to recording the minutiae of everyday life. For it is this sheer wealth of visual data, the painstaking chronicle of changes in dress, transport, street layouts, buildings, housing, engineering and landscape that captivates us so much today. His remarkable images offer us a powerful link with the past and with the lives of our ancestors.

TODAY'S TECHNOLOGY

Computers have now made it possible for Frith's many thousands of images to be accessed almost instantly. In the Frith archive today, each photograph is carefully 'digitised' then stored on a CD Rom. Frith archivists can locate a single photograph amongst thousands within seconds. Views can be catalogued and sorted under a variety of categories of place and content to the immediate benefit of researchers. Inexpensive reference prints can be created for them at the touch of a mouse button, and a wide range of books and other printed materials assembled and published for a wider, more general readership - in the next twelve months over a hundred Frith local history titles will be published! The

See Frith at www.francisfrith.com

day-to-day workings of the archive are very different from how they were in Francis Frith's time: imagine the herculean task of sorting through eleven tons of glass negatives as Frith had to do to locate a particular sequence of pictures! Yet the archive still prides itself on maintaining the same high standards of excellence laid down by Francis Frith, including the painstaking cataloguing and indexing of every view.

It is curious to reflect on how the internet now allows researchers in America and elsewhere greater instant access to the archive than Frith himself ever enjoyed. Many thousands of individual views can be called up on screen within seconds on one of the Frith internet sites, enabling people living continents away to revisit the streets of their ancestral home town, or view places in Britain where they have enjoyed holidays. Many overseas researchers welcome the chance to view special theme selections, such as transport, sports, costume and ancient monuments.

We are certain that Francis Frith would have heartily approved of these modern developments, for he himself was always working at the very limits of Victorian photographic technology.

THE VALUE OF THE ARCHIVE TODAY

Because of the benefits brought by the computer, Frith's images are increasingly studied by social historians, by researchers into genealogy and ancestory, by architects, town planners, and by teachers and schoolchildren involved in local history projects. In addition, the archive offers every one of us a unique opportunity to examine the places where we and our families have lived and worked down the years. Immensely successful in Frith's own era, the archive is now, a century and more on, entering a new phase of popularity.

THE PAST IN TUNE WITH THE FUTURE

Historians consider the Francis Frith Collection to be of prime national importance. It is the only archive of its kind remaining in private ownership and has been valued at a million pounds. However, this figure is now rapidly increasing as digital technology enables more and more people around the world to enjoy its benefits.

Francis Frith's archive is now housed in an historic timber barn in the beautiful village of Teffont in Wiltshire. Its founder would not recognize the archive office as it is today. In place of the many thousands of dusty boxes containing glass plate negatives and an all-pervading odour of photographic chemicals, there are now ranks of computer screens. He would be amazed to watch his images travelling round the world at unimaginable speeds through network and internet lines.

The archive's future is both bright and exciting. Francis Frith, with his unshakeable belief in making photographs available to the greatest number of people, would undoubtedly approve of what is being done today with his lifetime's work. His photographs, depicting our shared past, are now bringing pleasure and enlightenment to millions around the world a century and more after his death.

OXFORDSHIRE – *An Introduction*

VISITORS FROM FAR and wide have long been drawn to Oxford, one of Europe's most beautiful cities and renowned throughout the world as an ancient seat of learning. But what of the rest of the county?

Lying at the heart of England, Oxfordshire boasts a rich heritage and a surprisingly varied mix of scenery. Its landscape encompasses open chalk downlands and magnificent beechwoods, picturesque rivers and canals bustling with activity, ancient towns of mellow stone, and attractive villages set in peaceful farmland. In the south-west the county meets neighbouring Berkshire high on the downs, offering far-reaching vistas and fascinating links with the distant past. To the south-east lie the Chilterns, with their steep slopes and wooded hills providing a superb natural playground in this densely populated corner of the country. The countryside in the north-west of Oxfordshire, on the other hand, seems isolated by comparison, more redolent of the north of England, with its wide views, rolling hills and drystone walls, while historic Banbury acts as a gateway to the Midland counties.

As we enter the second millennium, we can look back and see how the strong influence of man has shaped this part of England over the centuries. The Romans built villas in the picturesque river valleys that thread their way through Oxfordshire, thhe Saxons constructed royal palaces here, and the Normans left their impressive legacy of castles and churches.

The philanthropic wool merchants made their mark, too, and many of their fine buildings still stand today, serving as a permanent reminder of what they did to benefit local communities. Like many of our English counties, Oxfordshire has also witnessed man's hunger for power and domination, symbolised by the ceaseless struggle over the years to possess the fertile lowland country to the north and south of the Thames. The county has had its battles too; it was stained by the blood of the defeated Danes in the 9th century and ravaged by the opposing armies of the English Civil War. The struggle for power and political supremacy has produced some of history's most prominent figures. One of Oxfordshire's boldest sons, Alfred the Great, was born at Wantage in AD 849. During his lifetime, the intrepid Alfred twice visited Rome, succeeded his brother as

King of Wessex and married into the ruling family of Mercia.

Alfred's powerful presence is still keenly felt in this corner of the county. He is everywhere. Even the chalk figure of the White Horse, on a hillside close to Alfred's birthplace, may have been cut to celebrate his victory over the Danes at the Battle of Ashdown in AD 871. At 365 feet long and 130 feet tall, the splendid outline of the galloping horse is best appreciated from some distance away. Nearby is the famous blowing stone, a block of brownish-red sarsen stone which originally stood high on the hills above the village of Kingston Lisle. It is claimed that blowing vigorously into a hole in the stone produces a memorable sound, not unlike that of a foghorn! Legend suggests that Alfred blew through it to rally his troops before doing battle with the Danes.

Crossing this wild, windswept downland country is the famous Ridgeway, quite possibly Britain's oldest road and now a popular long-distance trail. Traces of early man can be seen everywhere - Iron Age hillforts, burial mounds, sarsen stones and crumbling earthworks litter the landscape. This is a place of romantic legends and dramatic views. Although relatively new, the Ridgeway trail provides a unique insight into the changing character and rural heart of the county, as do Oxfordshire's other long-distance trails.

The majestic Thames, Oxfordshire's main artery of water, has been described as liquid history. Rising in a Gloucestershire meadow, the fledgling river drifts towards Oxford, then heads south for Abingdon, Wallingford and Goring where it forms the county's southern boundary. The Thames, historically one of the most important rivers in Britain, is known and loved throughout the world, and in its own way the Thames has helped mould the county's distinctive character through the centuries.

The Thames has been used as a highway since early times and a leisurely journey along it helps to put the river's relationship with the county into context. Meandering as it does

through this gentle landscape, the Thames passes many of Oxfordshire's most treasured landmarks, and, between Wallingford and Henley, the river is enhanced by some of the most beautiful scenery in the south of England. On the upper Thames, near the Gloucestershire border, lies the village of Kelmscott, famous as the summer home

Bablock Hythe, one of the most famous of all the Thames crossing points. The Romans crossed the river here and a ferry has been in service on and off for more than a thousand years. The 19th-century poet Matthew Arnold knew this place well and made references to Bablock Hythe and the surrounding countryside in his work. It was his Scholar

of William Morris, the 19th-century writer, craftsman and artist. Morris, a renowned idealist, wanted to achieve social harmony and create a kind of rural Utopia where men and women lived and worked together in perfect unison and there was no such thing as mass production. Morris died in 1896 and is buried in Kelmscott churchyard.

Further downstream is the tiny isolated community of Shifford, with its church standing out clearly amid the watermeadows. Evidence of old earthworks indicates that Shifford was a place of some importance. According to some sources, King Alfred was supposed to have conducted one of the earliest English parliaments here.

On the approach to Oxford, the river reaches

Gipsy who 'oft was met crossing the stripling Thames at Bablock-hythe'. Just to the east of the busy A34 lies the Trout Inn, a popular pub in the Oxford area and originally built as a hospice in the 12th century. Port Meadow, a vast expanse of ancient grazing land given by William the Conqueror to the burgesses of Oxford, provides teasing glimpses of 'that sweet city with her dreaming spires'. Arnold's exquisite words capture the beauty and grace of Oxford, likened by Thomas Hardy's Jude to 'the heavenly Jerusalem'.

South-east of Abingdon, which used to be the county town of Berkshire until Oxfordshire extended its boundaries in 1974, the river sweeps beneath the towering tree-crowned Sinodun Hills. These hills, better known locally as the Wittenham Clumps, rise almost 400 feet above the Thames. Castle Hill includes the earthworks of an Iron Age fort built to defend the river. Dorchester, on the north bank of the Thames, has a fascinating history. The Romans built a town here, though its ramparts are now only faintly identifiable.

Beyond the Goring Gap, where the Thames carved a new passage through the chalk hills during the last Ice Age, the river makes for Mapledurham Lock where classic river illustrations by a local artist can be seen and a sign on the island tells you that London is 78.5 miles away. Flowing serenely through Reading, the Thames heads north again to leave Oxfordshire by way of Henley, famous for its annual regatta which has been held in the town since the 19th century.

I have barely touched on the county in this introduction. Much of Oxfordshire remains undiscovered by the camera-clicking tourist - particularly the coach parties who invade Oxford, Woodstock, Blenheim Palace and the Cotswolds. We may be thankful that there is so much more to the county than these obvious attractions, but only by exploring a complex network of towns and villages can you fully appreciate the real Oxfordshire. Francis Frith's social record of the county, captured in a series of fascinating photographs, helps us to understand what changes have occurred within Oxfordshire's boundaries during the last one hundred years or so. And there have certainly been many changes. A way of life that was once the very fabric of rural and urban Britain has all but disappeared; if Francis Frith were to come back today, he would undoubtedly find the modern world very confusing.

As we enter a new millennium, many aspects of our daily lives seem uncertain or under threat. Change is not always for the better, and, as if to compensate for any upheaval that we have to endure, we invariably allow ourselves to wallow in a golden glow of nostalgia, relying on our memories to recall a time when life seemed simpler, slower and less stressful than today. But whatever happens in the future, Frith's images - sometimes amusing, sometimes stark and sometimes thought-provoking but never less than captivating - will always be there to provide us with a unique and compelling insight into life as it used to be. That is why the importance of his archive can never be underestimated.

WANTAGE, MARKET PLACE c1950 W251006
The market town of Wantage is famous as the birthplace of King Alfred, who was born here in 849 AD. The striking marble statue of the King, in the middle of the Market Place, was carved by Count Gleichen and presented to the town by Lord Wantage in 1877.

WANTAGE, THE MARKET PLACE AND THE TOWN HALL c1955 W251011
Note the variety of architectural styles in this corner of the Market Place. The building on the right is timber-framed and infilled with herringbone brickwork. Next to the Bell Inn is Tesco, describing itself as the 'Modern Grocers' - a far cry from today's image of the famous store.

WANTAGE, MARKET PLACE C1955 W251056
Peeping into view on the left of the picture is the sturdy tower of Wantage parish church, which dates from the late 13th century and was restored by the distinguished local architect George Street in 1857. The church commemorates several members of the Fitzwarren family who were related by marriage to Dick Whittington.

WANTAGE, THE MARKET PLACE C1965 W251076
The blue and red brick buildings on the extreme right of the photograph serve as perfect examples of the regional building style of the 18th century. Most of the present town dates from the 17th and 18th centuries.

ASHBURY, THE SCHOOL 1919 A98001
A charming village scene captured for posterity the
year after the First World War finally ended. The
remote downland village of Ashbury is situated
between the Vale of the White Horse and the
Lambourn Downs, close to the Wiltshire border.

FARINGDON, THE MARKET PLACE c1955 F94021

King Alfred had a royal manor here and King John granted the town a charter for a weekly market. Many of the buildings are limestone; the old Town Hall is worth a look, as are the Georgian facades of the inns in the Market Place.

SHRIVENHAM, THE MEMORIAL HALL c1960 S350037

The village lies in the far west of the county, close to the Wiltshire border. Village halls and memorial halls have long been an integral part of the local community, providing a venue for public meetings and social functions.

SHRIVENHAM, BECKETT HALL ROYAL MILITARY COLLEGE OF SCIENCE C1960 S350047
Beckett Hall was acquired by the War Office in 1938 for use as an Artillery School. However, during the Second World War it became an Officer Cadet Training Unit. Up to 10,000 US troops were based in the area, and after the war Beckett Hall became the United States Forces University in Europe. It is now the Royal Military College of Science.

EYNSHAM, HIGH STREET c1955 E92008
E M Mumford, on the corner of the High Street and the Market Square, displayed enamel trade signs on its gable end when this photograph was taken in the mid 1950s. Further down the street is a van with 'Lyons Tea, Coffee & Cocoa' emblazoned on its rear door.

EYNSHAM, HIGH STREET c1965 E92016
Originally the property of the Anglo Saxon kings of Mercia in the 8th century, Eynsham later became the setting for a Benedictine abbey which stood near the present church. Little remains of it today. The market town is reached over a toll bridge built by Lord Abingdon in 1769.

WITNEY, MARKET SQUARE C1955 W256017

Witney, in the west of the county, has long been famous for its links with the wool trade, as well as the manufacture of blankets, which have been produced here for over 700 years. The market was held around the 17th-century Buttercross in the centre of the town.

BURFORD, HIGH STREET c1955 B369011
Often described as the gateway to the
Cotswolds, the picturesque town of Burford
has changed little over the years. The High
Street runs down between pollarded lime
trees and mellow stone houses to the river
Windrush. Charles II stayed here, possibly
with Nell Gwynn, whose child was named the
Earl of Burford.

CHIPPING NORTON, HIGH STREET c1960 C288063
Chipping Norton - or 'Chippy' as the locals call it - prospered as a result of the wool trade. The highest town in Oxfordshire boasts a striking High Street; St Mary's Church and many of the town's handsome buildings were built by prosperous wool merchants.

CHIPPING NORTON, HIGH STREET c1955 C288037
Chipping Norton's imposing Town Hall can be seen in this 1950s photograph. The building, which is mid 19th-century and stands on the site of the old Market Hall, faces away from the town's wide Market Place. A stone pillar remains as a relic of the old hall.

CHIPPING NORTON, BLISS TWEED MILLS C1960 C288051
On the outskirts of Chipping Norton lies the Victorian tweed mill, founded by the Bliss family in the 18th century for the manufacture of linsey woolseys, kersey webs, horse cloth, serges and tweeds. The mill was rebuilt following a fire in 1872.

GREAT TEW, THE VILLAGE c1960 G130010

GREAT TEW
The Village c1960
Historian Arthur Mee, in his book 'The King's England - Oxfordshire,' says that 'if our England is a garden Great Tew is one of its rare plots...never anything but beautiful'. Great Tew was originally designed as an estate village in the 19th century, with the intention of blending architectural beauty with utility and agricultural management.

BLOXHAM
Old Bridge Road c1955
The hilltop village of Bloxham has a striking parish church with an intricately designed late 14th-century tower and spire, possibly completed by the same masons who worked on neighbouring Adderbury church. The two spires, along with that of King's Sutton, are described in the following lines: 'Bloxham for length, Adderbury for strength, And King's Sutton for beauty'.

BLOXHAM, OLD BRIDGE ROAD c1955 B367008

ADDERBURY, HIGH STREET c1955 A139001
Adderbury, south of Banbury, evolved as a result of the wool trade. Lord Montagu, William of Orange's minister, lived here at one time. The sturdy spire of St Mary's church is visible for miles around. Note the old Hovis sign just below it.

BROUGHTON, THE CASTLE 1922 72110

Broughton Castle was built as a fortified manor house by Sir John de Broughton in the 14th century. It was later acquired by William of Wykeham who converted the house into a castle. In the 15th century Broughton passed by marriage to the Fiennes family, and during the Elizabethan era the house was transformed into the Tudor building you see today.

BANBURY, MARKET PLACE 1921 70571

Banbury once boasted a castle which enabled the town to grow in the shadow of its protective walls. However, Banbury suffered greatly during the Civil War and the castle was completely destroyed in 1648. This photograph shows a corner of the Market Place to the right of the cinema.

BANBURY, OLD HOUSES, MARKET PLACE 1922 72090
The silent film version of 'The Count of Monte Cristo' was showing when this photograph was taken. The cinema has a strong Gothic look to it. Garden mowers can be seen lined up outside the premises of Robins Brothers, ironmongers.

BANBURY, MARKET PLACE 1921 70572
Banbury's spacious Market Place is overlooked by many buildings of different
architectural styles. The cinema is now a bank. On the right of it are the premises of
Titcombe & Sons, wholesale and family grocers. Several milk carts can be seen in the
picture and on the right are some hay rakes and tin baths.

BANBURY, THE TOWN HALL 1921 70573

The second largest town in Oxfordshire, Banbury has long been famous as the main meeting point of routes from the Midlands to London and Oxford. The splendid Town Hall, which dominates the picture, was designed in the Gothic style of the 15th century and opened in 1854. The clock was added later.

BANBURY, MARKET PLACE c1960 B13071

The clock on the top of the Town Hall is visible, peeping above the rooftops in the town's Market Place. Nathan's Domestic Stores can be seen on the right and the office of Prudential Assurance Company at the far end.

BANBURY, PARSONS STREET 1921 70576
Ye Olde Reinedeer Inn is famous for the Globe Room, a Civil War meeting place. The splendid 17th-century panelling from this room was rescued from a London warehouse and returned to Banbury in the 1970s.

BANBURY, HIGH STREET 1921 70574

The old AA logo can be seen above the sign for the Red Lion. The inn looks across the High Street to Boots Cash Chemists and Stationers. An auction notice on the left of the picture advertises a sale of five hundred sheets of corrugated iron and imported timber.

BANBURY, THE OXFORD CANAL 1921 70593

The Oxford Canal, one of Britain's earliest inland waterways, took 20 years to complete and was finished in 1790. Beginning near Coventry, it never extended south of Oxford, where it joins the Thames. In its day, the canal played a key role in the transportation of coal.

CROPREDY, THE LOCK c1960 C291015
The name 'cropredy' is thought to come from Old English - 'redy' meaning brook. The village lies on the banks of the Oxford Canal and the river Cherwell. A bloody Civil War battle took place near here in 1644.

CROPREDY, THE OXFORD CANAL c1960 C291006

CROPREDY
The Oxford Canal c1960
Some of the soldiers who were killed in the furious battle of 1644 are buried in the village churchyard. Various sources suggest that the people of Cropredy, fearing for the church possessions, seized an exquisite eagle lectern and hurled it into the river to prevent enemy forces from snatching it. The eagle was recovered 30 years later.

BICESTER
Market Square c1955
Note the interesting variety of architectural styles, including gabled houses with tiled roofs, in Bicester's three-cornered Market Square. Sadly, several 18th-century fires destroyed many of the town's old timber buildings. The Market Square, the hub of Bicester, still retains the feel of a country town.

BICESTER, MARKET SQUARE c1955 B365001

WOODSTOCK, MARKET PLACE c1965 W258117

The town of Woodstock was once a favourite manor and hunting lodge for English kings. The Black Prince was born here. Various striking Georgian buildings overlook the Market Place, and there are many hotels and inns hereabouts, including the Bear Hotel, on the right of the picture, which dates back to the 13th century.

WOODSTOCK, MARKET PLACE AND TOWN HALL c1955 W258016

One of Woodstock's most imposing buildings is the 18th-century Town Hall, built in classical style by Sir William Chambers and paid for by the Duke of Marlborough. The building looks out across the Market Place to Park Street.

WOODSTOCK, MARKET STREET c1955 W258121

A Royal Blue coach bound for Liverpool pulls into Market Street. The Cotswold-stone Dorchester Hotel, seen on the extreme left of the photograph, opened in 1947. After extensive refurbishment, it reopened as the Feathers in the 1980s. The 17th-century building was originally four separate houses.

WOODSTOCK, OXFORD STREET 1950 W258019

Woodstock's close proximity to Blenheim Palace has long made it one of Britain's most popular destinations. The town has been attracting visitors for nearly 300 years; in the 1950s, when this photograph was taken, there were many hotels, tearooms and guest houses to cater for the large numbers of tourists.

WOODSTOCK, PARK STREET AND CHAUCER'S HOUSE c1955 W258015
The aptly named Woodstock Gate, one of the main entrances to Blenheim Palace, lies just around the corner. The view from the gate of the palace and its parkland is often described as the finest in England. Chaucer lived in the house which has shutters, and a circular window on the first floor.

KIDLINGTON, THE CROSS ROADS c1955 K85017

KIDLINGTON
The Cross Roads c1955
Kidlington Garden City developed as a dormitory commuter settlement in the 1930s. The old village lies to the east of the Banbury road, and the magnificent 15th-century church spire is visible from miles around. The Britannia Inn, a Morrell's pub, can be seen next to the grocer's.

◆

THAME
Corn Market 1951
This classic market town is famous for its broad streets and many inns - The Black Horse can be seen on the left in the picture. The most notable hostelry is the Spread Eagle, which was acquired by John Fothergill in 1922. During the next ten years Fothergill transformed the inn beyond recognition, offering his favourite clients - including Graham Greene and Evelyn Waugh - a unique and impeccable service.

THAME, CORN MARKET 1951 T106011

IFFLEY
The Mill Lock & Bridge 1890

The village of Iffley has been swallowed up by Oxford, though its true heart remains intact. Iffley Mill, first mentioned in 1106, was destroyed by fire in 1908. The lock was the first of three pound locks, or turnpikes as they used to be known, built on the river in 1632.

◆

OXFORD
Christ Church College 1890

Christ Church, the largest college in Oxford, was founded in 1525 by Cardinal Wolsey. When he was disgraced it was refounded as King Henry VIII College. Later it became known as Christ Church when the college and the cathedral became one. Over the years Christ Church has had many notable students, including three prime ministers: Robert Peel, William Gladstone and Lord Salisbury. John Wesley, Lewis Carroll and W H Auden also studied here.

IFFLEY, THE MILL LOCK & BRIDGE 1890 26959

OXFORD, CHRIST CHURCH COLLEGE 1890 26813

OXFORD, CHRIST CHURCH 1922 72009
The cathedral's official title is 'The Cathedral Church of Christ in Oxford'. Not only is it the smallest of all English cathedrals, but it is also the college chapel of Christ Church - making it unique in the history of Oxford.

OXFORD, CHRIST CHURCH, TOM TOWER 1890 26815
Tom Tower is one of the college's most treasured architectural features, as well as a famous landmark on the Oxford skyline. John Fell, Dean of Christ Church and Bishop of Oxford, engaged Christopher Wren to crown the main gateway with this splendid creation, transferring the medieval bell from the cathedral to the college.

OXFORD, CHRIST CHURCH TOWER 1890 26829
Christ Church is renowned for its magnificent hall, impressive timbered roof and collection of portraits, including Henry VIII and Cardinal Wolsey. When John Fell was Dean of Christ Church, one of his students based a famous Latin epigram on him following a reprimand.

OXFORD, MAGDALEN COLLEGE & RIVER CHERWELL c1950 033110
The college, founded in 1458 by William Waynflete, sits on the banks of the Cherwell, one of Oxfordshire's prettiest rivers. On the left is the University Botanic Garden, founded in 1621 by the Earl of Danby and established on the site of a 13th-century Jewish burial ground.

OXFORD, MAGDALEN COLLEGE FROM THE BRIDGE 1938 88122

OXFORD
Magdalen College from the Bridge 1938
During the Civil War Royalist forces defended Magdalen Bridge by throwing rocks from the top of the bell tower down on the heads of Parliamentarians below. The tower, which signifies the eastern entrance to the High Street, was begun in 1492 and took seventeen years to complete, almost certainly because of ongoing financial difficulties.

◆

OXFORD
Magdalen College 1890
A classic Victorian picture of Oxford, which shows a punt on the Cherwell and the striking Perpendicular bell tower of Magdalen College in the background. On May morning, the college choristers and the dons assemble at the top of the tower to sing a Latin hymn.

OXFORD, MAGDALEN COLLEGE 1890 26819

OXFORD
Brasenose College Quadrangle 1890 26885
The college was founded in 1509 and takes its name from the
form of an ancient brass door-knocker. According to some
sources, the original brazen nose was carried off by rebellious
students to Brasenose Hall at Stamford in Lincolnshire, a rival
seat of learning. It remained there until 1890. The gateway
dates from the college's foundation. This Victorian photograph
shows Brasenose College standing in the shadow of the
Radcliffe Camera, which became one of the reading rooms for
the Bodleian Library 30 years before this picture was taken.

OXFORD, BALLIOL COLLEGE WITH TRINITY COLLEGE 1922 72020
Balliol, which claims to be the oldest of all the Oxford colleges, was
endowed in 1265. The controversial Gothic buildings, designed by
Alfred Waterhouse, overlook Broad Street and date from the 1860s.
Trinity College, Balliol's neighbour, was founded in 1555.

OXFORD, BALLIOL COLLEGE 1922 72017

'It is fitting that Balliol, the most progressive of our colleges, should have so large a proportion of its buildings modern', wrote Dr Wells in 1897. Until the early 19th century Balliol's reputation was flawed: the place was dismissed as a 'dear, dim, drinking college'. Open scholarships and clever tutors helped transform Balliol's image.

OXFORD, BALLIOL COLLEGE 1890 26905

Balliol College was founded by John de Balliol. Many distinguished figures have passed through its hallowed halls - among them Matthew Arnold, Graham Greene, Harold Macmillan and Edward Heath. Most of Balliol's buildings, by Salvin and Butterfield, are 19th-century.

OXFORD, BALLIOL COLLEGE & THE MARTYRS' MEMORIAL 1900 45455
To the right of Balliol College is the famous Martyrs' Memorial, commemorating the 16th-century Protestant martyrs Latimer, Ridley and Cranmer, who were burned at the stake in nearby Broad Street. A plaque on the front of the college marks the spot.

OXFORD, THE MARTYRS' MEMORIAL 1922 72027
The memorial in St Giles dates back to 1841; it stands on an island in the road and was designed by George Gilbert Scott. Behind it is the Church of St Mary Magdalen. To the right is the imposing front of the famous Randolph Hotel.

OXFORD, HIGH STREET 1922 71992
On the right of the picture is the splendid facade of Queen's College,
a striking classical building designed by Christopher Wren's pupil,
Hawksmoor. The first stone was laid in 1710, on Queen Anne's birthday.
Beneath the cupola above the central gateway, though it is not clearly
visible, is a statue of Caroline, Queen of George II, who donated £1,000
towards the completion of the quadrangle.

OXFORD, HIGH STREET 1922 71989
The graceful 14th-century spire of St Mary the Virgin Church, rising to nearly two hundred feet, dominates this photograph of the High Street. The tower is 13th-century. Note the cars and the fashions, which are typically 1920s.

OXFORD, HIGH STREET 1900 45182
Although nothing remains of it today, there was a St Mary's Church here in the 11th century, which at that time was the most famous building in Oxford. The present church contains a memorial to Dr John Radcliffe, one of Oxford's greatest benefactors and most famous figures.

OXFORD, HIGH STREET 1890 26912
Queen's College is named after Philippa, wife of Edward III, whose chaplain founded the college. It was originally intended to educate 'poor boys' from the north of England. However, all that changed when one of them, Joseph Williamson, became Secretary of State and transformed the college into the building you see today.

OXFORD, HIGH STREET 1937 88069
This photograph shows the famous High Street, generally regarded as one of the most beautiful streets in Europe. When walking its length from east to west, you can appreciate the sweeping curve which gradually reveals some of Oxford's most striking buildings.

OXFORD, HIGH STREET 1900 45183

Rising above the High Street are the tower and delicate spire of All Saints' Church, built in the 18th century to replace a Norman church which was destroyed when the spire collapsed on top of it in 1699. The spire, a distinctive feature of the Oxford skyline, was designed by Hawksmoor. No longer a church, All Saints' is now the library of Lincoln College.

OXFORD, QUEENS COLLEGE FRONT QUADRANGLE 1890 26924

The Front Quadrangle, seen here, dates back to 1710-34 and is based in part on designs by Hawksmoor. The Hall and Chapel are crowned by a small domed tower, beneath which is an ornately carved pediment with symbolic figures of Justice, Neptune and Plenty.

OXFORD, BROAD STREET 1897 40021
Two of Oxford's most famous colleges, Trinity and Balliol, stand on the left side of Broad Street, famous for its bookshops, among which is Blackwell's. In the distance is the classical facade of the Clarendon Building, formerly the administrative heart of the University.

OXFORD, BROAD STREET 1890 26942
To the right of this photograph is the Sheldonian Theatre, designed by Christopher Wren and opened in 1669.
The Theatre, named after Gilbert Sheldon, the 17th-century Archbishop of Canterbury, was built as an assembly
hall for University occasions and is still used for meetings and concerts.

OXFORD, ST GILES c1950 O33112
On the east side of St Giles is St John's College, founded in 1437 for Cistercian monks. To the west, screened by
trees, is a famous Oxford pub, The Eagle and Child, which during the Civil War became a payhouse for the Royalist
Army. J R R Tolkien and C S Lewis met here every week during the 1940s and 50s.

OXFORD, ST GILES 1890 26914
On the extreme left of the picture is the Taylor Institute.
The Taylorian, dedicated to the study of modern languages at the
University, is characterised by statues symbolising the languages of
France, Italy, Germany and Spain, and was founded with a bequest
from Sir Robert Taylor, an 18th-century architect.

OXFORD, SOMERVILLE COLLEGE 1907 57393
Founded for women 28 years before this photograph was taken, Somerville College is barely visible from the street. Named after Mary Somerville, a Scottish mathematician, the college boasts two prime ministers among its graduates - Indira Gandhi and Margaret Thatcher.

OXFORD, HERTFORD COLLEGE 1906 53700
Hertford College dates back to 1284 when it was founded as Hart Hall. The Hall was incorporated as a college by Royal Charter in the middle of the 18th century, though by the mid 19th century it had fallen into decay. However, its fortunes were later revived by Act of Parliament.

OXFORD, LINCOLN COLLEGE 1906 53698

OXFORD
Lincoln College 1906

The college was founded in 1427 by Richard Fleming, Bishop of Lincoln. However, lack of funds prevented the college from being finished: at the time of the Bishop's death in 1431, only the gate tower and staircase had been completed. Various benefactors, including John Forest, Dean of Wells, came to the rescue, and work on the college was eventually finished.

◆

OXFORD
New College Entrance Gateway 1902

Founded in 1379 by William of Wykeham, New College includes one of the oldest quadrangles in Oxford. The gatehouse was where the Warden used to monitor the comings and goings of his students. The college gardens are bordered on two sides by the ancient city wall.

OXFORD, NEW COLLEGE ENTRANCE GATEWAY 1902 48626

OXFORD, ST ALDATES c1950 O33137

St Aldates is one of Oxford's most famous thoroughfares. Christ Church, otherwise known as 'The House', can be seen on the right, with Wren's splendid Tom Tower rising above it. Note the old bus stop sign on the right, and how quiet the street seems compared with today's heavy traffic.

OXFORD, ST ALDATES CHURCH 1890 26945

Originally a Saxon church, St Aldates was rebuilt in 1004. Following the Dissolution of the Monastries, it was acquired by the Crown before becoming part of Pembroke College. Its members worshipped here until the college built its own chapel in 1732.

OXFORD, QUEEN STREET c1950 O33124
Until it was demolished at the end of the 19th century, St Martin's Church stood on this site. The heavily restored medieval tower is all that remains. St Martin's was the city church and a meeting point in times of war and victory. There is a memorable view of Oxford from the top.

OXFORD, CORNMARKET STREET c1950 O33129
This photograph shows Cornmarket Street running down to Carfax, with the outline of Tom Tower dominating St Aldates on the far side. The premises of Barclays Bank can be seen on the right, next door to Morris Garages.

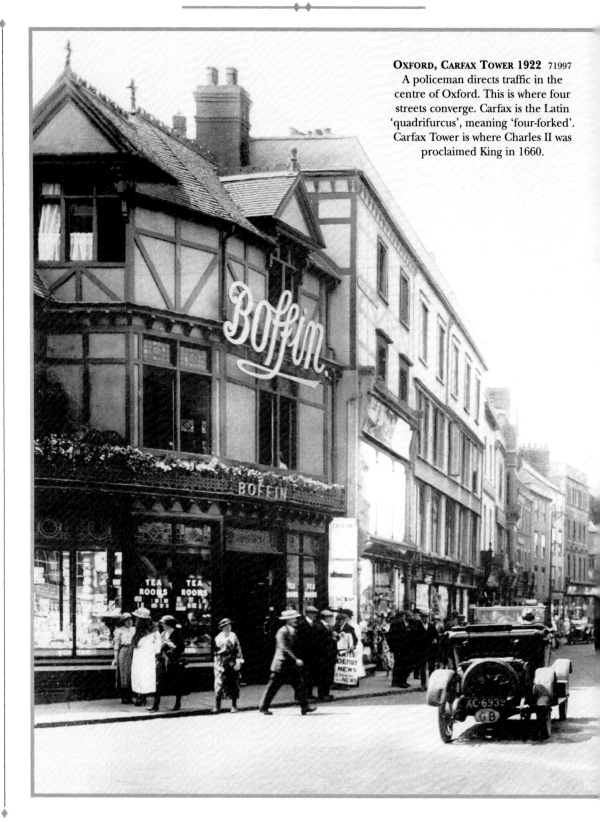

OXFORD, CARFAX TOWER 1922 71997
A policeman directs traffic in the
centre of Oxford. This is where four
streets converge. Carfax is the Latin
'quadrifurcus', meaning 'four-forked'.
Carfax Tower is where Charles II was
proclaimed King in 1660.

OXFORD
Cornmarket Street 1922 71996
The 11th-century Saxon tower of St Michael's Church is clearly
seen on the right of Cornmarket Street. Until 1771, the North
Gate of Oxford spanned the Cornmarket beside this tower.
This was also the site of the Bocardo prison, where the Oxford
Martyrs were held.

OXFORD, CORNMARKET STREET 1922 71995
A motorbike and side car can be seen heading towards St Michael's Church, where John Wesley preached from the 15th-century pulpit in 1726. The chancel is 13th-century, and the tower is thought to be the oldest surviving building in Oxford. On the left is the old Clarendon Hotel.

OXFORD, FROM CARFAX TOWER 1922 71986
Much of Oxford, 'that sweet city with her dreaming spires', can be seen in this splendid photograph captured from the top of Carfax Tower. Among the most prominent landmarks are the Radcliffe Camera and the spire of All Saints Church.

OXFORD, CARFAX 1937 88074

To the left of Carfax there used to be a 'pennyless bench' where beggars sat and women sold butter. Over 300 years before this picture was taken, the huge Carfax Conduit was built in the middle of the junction, conveying piped water from nearby Hinksey.

OXFORD, FROM CARFAX TOWER 1922 71988

Oxford's superb Town Hall building dominates this picture of the city centre. At the bottom of the photograph is Queen Street, named after Queen Charlotte, wife of George III. Many of the street's medieval buildings have disappeared over the years.

OXFORD, THE RIVER FROM FOLLY BRIDGE 1890 26948
Here we see steamers and pleasure craft on the Thames at Oxford. This photograph was taken from Folly Bridge, which originally had a tower and gatehouse. Known as Friar Bacon's study, it was used by Roger Bacon, the 13th-century astronomer and scientist, as an observatory. Bacon also used the church tower at nearby Sunningwell to make astronomical observations.

OXFORD, COLLEGE BARGES 1890 26951
This scenic stretch of the Thames, by Christ Church Meadow, has long been a rowing reach; at one time the bank would have been lined with eye-catching college barges, which were used as clubhouses and grandstands. Sadly, they have gone - most of them have fallen into decay or have been converted into modest houses or holiday accommodation.

OXFORD, ST PETER'S IN THE EAST 1890 26946
This is one of Oxford's secret gems. The lesser-known St Peter's in the East is a fascinating old church which lies hidden beyond St Edmund Hall. The church, which contains a vaulted Norman crypt beneath the chancel, stands in the shadow of New College Garden.

OXFORD, THE DIVINITY SCHOOL 1907 57372

The Divinity School dates back to the 15th century, and was built to provide a theological lecture room. Its most prominent feature is the magnificent vaulted roof exquisitely decorated with figures and coats of arms. The Oxford Martyrs were cited to appear for examination here. It was later used as a corn store before being renovated by Wren.

OXFORD, THE UNION CLUB 1890 26943

The Oxford Union consists of various buildings in the style of the Gothic Revival which date back to the Victorian and Edwardian eras. William Morris, who, among others, painted the library frescoes, is said to have dined at Christ Church with his hair splattered with blue paint. The Union is used by undergraduates for political debate.

OXFORD, THE CASTLE 1912 64171

OXFORD
The Castle 1912

The late Norman tower of Oxford Castle overlooks a branch of the river which cuts between various small factories and dilapidated buildings. Within the castle precincts lie a Saxon mound and a Norman crypt.

OXFORD
The Plain 1922

The Plain, as it is known, lies just to the east of Magdalen Bridge, representing the boundary of the old city. Here the Cherwell flows under the easterly part of the High Street. Nearby Magdalen College is the first significant building you see on entering the city by the old London road.

OXFORD, THE PLAIN 1922 71998

OXFORD, THE CHERWELL 1906 53704A
Hemmed in by a circle of hills and built on a gravel bank between the Thames Isis and the Cherwell, Oxford gives the impression of sitting on an island. The damp climate here probably drove the Romans away.

OXFORD, ON THE CHERWELL 1912 64172

OXFORD
On the Cherwell 1912
Adjoining the Cherwell is the great
green expanse of Christ Church
Meadow, which is held in trust by Christ
Church and was originally given by Lady
Montacute to maintain her Chantry
in the Lady Chapel at the Priory of St
Frideswide (Christ Church Cathedral).

OXFORD
View of the Cherwell 1906
The Cherwell is a peaceful backwater
where visitors and locals can enjoy the
tranquil scene and yet remain within
the shadow of the city. Wordsworth was
inspired by the view of Christ Church
Meadow, which is enhanced by the river,
the spires and the magnificent
college buildings.

OXFORD, VIEW OF THE CHERWELL 1906 53705

OXFORD, COWLEY 1890 26803
When this picture was taken in the Victorian era, Cowley was a large village gradually being swallowed up by the suburbs of Oxford. Later, Cowley was to change forever when the motor industry began to envelop this corner of the city in the early years of the 20th century.

OXFORD, THE MARSTON FERRY 1912 64174
Children crossing the river at Marston, once a village but now a north Oxford suburb. During the Civil War, the old manor house was the headquarters of the Parliamentarian army. A cannonball fired from here struck the north wall of Christ Church, where Charles I and his court were staying at the time.

BENSON, HIGH STREET C1965 B364049

BENSON
High Street c1965
Famous for its RAF station, Benson grew during the turnpike and coaching era. The village became well known for several popular coaching inns, the Georgian Castle, the White Hart and the Crown, which is seen on the right. A spitfire based at Benson spotted the 'Bismarck' near Bergen in 1941.

BENSON
Brook Street c1955
Bensington is Benson's proper name; it was once an ancient British city. A battle was fought here in 572 AD between the West Saxons and the Britons. In 775 AD the Mercians defeated Cynewulf, King of Wessex in this area.

BENSON, BROOK STREET C1955 B364039

WALLINGFORD, MARKET PLACE C1965 W10136
The striking tower of St Mary's Church looks out across Wallingford's picturesque Market Place. Much of the church was rebuilt during the 19th century. In front of the Town Hall is a war memorial unveiled in 1921. Wallingford was granted a charter in 1155.

WALLINGFORD, MARKET PLACE AND THE CHURCH 1893 31711
Wallingford's imposing 17th-century Town Hall dominates this Victorian photograph. The building rests on pillars; it contains portraits by Lawrence and Gainsborough, as well as a silver mace and the 15th-century town seal. On the left is the 19th-century Corn Exchange, now a theatre.

WALLINGFORD, MARKET PLACE 1893 31712

The Victorian drinking fountain at the far end of the Market Place was given to Wallingford in 1885 by Alderman Hawkins, who ran a draper's shop, Field and Hawkins, in the town.

WALLINGFORD, THE BRIDGE BOAT HOUSE 1899 42988

William the Conqueror crossed the river here in 1066. On the left of the picture is the long 900-ft bridge of sixteen arches, and on the opposite bank is the Town Arms. To the right is the Bridge Boat House and landing stage, now a restaurant.

WALLINGFORD, THE CHURCH AND THE BRIDGE 1899 42986
Here we see the serene Thames at Wallingford. Peeping into view is St Peter's Church, characterised by a hollow, needle-like spire. The church, rebuilt in 1769-77, contains the tomb of Sir William Blackstone, Oxford's first professor of law, who presented St Peter's with a clock from Horseguards in London.

WALLINGFORD, FROM THE RIVER 1893 31709
The Anglo-Saxons almost certainly fortified Wallingford, and there was once an important castle here, though little of it survives today. The town was the last Royalist stronghold to surrender during the Civil War. At one time Wallingford had 16 churches.

SHILLINGFORD, THE SWAN HOTEL 1890 27018
The three-arched, balustraded bridge at Shillingford dates back to 1827 and carries the Wallingford to Thame road over the river. The road was turnpiked in 1764. The old wharf is a fascinating local feature. A couple of miles upstream is the confluence of the Thames and the Thame.

GORING, THE VILLAGE 1896 38307
This sprawling riverside village lies between the beech-clad hills of the Chilterns and the windswept slopes of the Berkshire Downs. Plenty of large Victorian houses and ornate villas can be seen in this photograph of Goring. Excavations undertaken in 1892-93 revealed a medieval priory on the east and south side of the parish church.

GORING, THE VILLAGE 1899 42991
The ivy-clad inn on the left of the photograph is the Miller of Mansfield, a famous pub in the Thames Valley. The coming of the railway and Goring's close proximity to the river helped put the village on the map around the turn of the century.

GORING, THATCHED COTTAGES 1896 38310
The village is a mixture of brick and flint thatched
cottages and more modern Victorian and Edwardian
villas. Goring is situated in a gap cut through the
Chilterns by the Thames during the last Ice Age.

GORING, THE LOCK 1896 38312
Goring-on-Thames is famous for its rather complex series of locks and weirs which are designed to control the river's water level and allow the passage of pleasure craft. The village's scenic Thames-side setting made it a popular haunt of the Victorians and the Edwardians, and it continues to be favoured by visitors today.

GORING, THE LOCK 1896 38313
Goring was an important settlement in prehistoric times, and it was here at the ford that the famous Ridgeway and Icknield Way joined forces. Across the river is neighbouring Streatley, linked to Goring by an old wooden bridge until it was replaced in the 1920s.

GORING, THE LOCK 1896 38314

Boathouses line the river here. A tragic accident occurred here in 1674 when a ferry overturned and sixty people were drowned. Centuries ago drovers herded sheep and cattle across the river at this point.

WATLINGTON c1955 W254006

The small town of Watlington, at the foot of the Chiltern escarpment, used to be famous for its many inns. However, all that changed when a 19th-century Methodist acquired six of them and immediately closed them down.

WATLINGTON, THE TOWN HALL c1955 W254023
The town's focal point is its gabled Town Hall, constructed in 1664 and standing by itself in the middle of the triangular Market Place. At one time a bridge connected the Town Hall to the upper floors of the Hare & Hounds, seen on the left.

HENLEY-ON-THAMES, THE BRIDGE 1890 27191
Records indicate that there has been a bridge spanning the Thames at Henley since 1234. The present bridge was built by William Hayward: it is decorated with carved masks on the keystones showing Father Thames looking through bulrushes downstream and Isis looking upstream.

HENLEY-ON-THAMES, MARKET PLACE 1893 31732
From the beginning, Henley's prosperity depended on communications. Timber, stone, corn and malt were transported from here to London by river. Its 18th-century economy depended on the coaching trade; further expansion followed the dawning of the railway age. The Town Hall was built to commemorate the Diamond Jubilee of Queen Victoria.

HENLEY-ON-THAMES, HART STREET 1893 31733
The central position of its parish church and the rectilinear layout of the town, which can still be traced today, are remnants of medieval planning. St Mary's distinctive tower was probably built by Bishop Longland - a native of Henley - who was Bishop of Lincoln from 1521-47.

HENLEY-ON-THAMES, THE REGATTA 1890 27203
Henley is famous for its Royal Regatta, held during the first week in July. The first Henley Royal Regatta was held in June 1839 and has been an important event in the town's social calendar ever since.

HENLEY-ON-THAMES, THE REGATTA 1890 27207
Ten years before the annual Royal Regatta began, the first Oxford and Cambridge University boat race was held on the Thames at Henley. It was an inauspicious start for Cambridge, as they lost the race. The venue later switched to West London.

HENLEY-ON-THAMES, REGATTA DAY 1899 43017
The aim of the Royal Regatta was to boost the local economy and to provide entertainment. It was so successful that it was established in 1851 under the patronage of the Prince Consort. Many other events and races have since been added.

HENLEY-ON-THAMES, THE REGATTA 1890 27200
The world-famous regatta takes place on a scenic stretch of the Thames
between Henley Bridge and Temple Island, site of an elegant Georgian folly.
The course is 1 mile and 450 yards long. Rowing upstream, as the oarsmen
do, provides splendid views of the bridge and the church tower.

HENLEY-ON-THAMES, REGATTA DAY 1899 43020
Hundreds of spectators line the Thames riverbank on Regatta Day in this late-Victorian photograph. There are also launches for hire and boats to let, as the sign advertises. By the turn of the century, the event had become one of the major attractions of the English Season.

SHIPLAKE, THE MILL AND LOCK 1890 27166
The river Loddon meets the Thames at Shiplake. Alexander Pope described the river thus: 'The Loddon slow, with silver alders crown'd'. Shiplake is situated on a chalk cliff, prettily overhanging one of the loveliest bends of the river.

SHIPLAKE, THE MILL AND LOCK 1890 27167
The Thames falls by three feet and six inches at Shiplake Lock. Alfred Tennyson was married in Shiplake church in 1850. His bride was Emily Sellwood, whom Tennyson had known since she was a girl of seventeen.

**MAPLEDURHAM
THE MILL 1890** 27091
This delightful photograph
depicts Mapledurham's
15th-century corn mill,
which is distinguished
by an undershot wooden
wheel. Two pairs of
millstones are used to
produce wholemeal
flour; today this restored
building is the only
working watermill left on
the Thames.

MAPLEDURHAM, THE LOCK 1890 27088
The scene here has hardly changed at all since this photograph was taken more than one hundred years ago. The timeless Thames presents an idyllic picture, with the river meandering between lazy meadows and spectacular chalk hillsides.

MAPLEDURHAM, THE LOCK 1890 27089
Two fine country houses lie close by. Mapledurham House was completed during the 16th century by Sir Richard Blount for his Catholic family, while further upstream is Hardwick House, a gabled Tudor mansion where Elizabeth I stayed and Charles I played bowls on the lawn.

WHITCHURCH, THE ROYAL OAK 1899 43002
Whitchurch lies opposite Pangbourne, which is situated on the Berkshire bank. This turn-of-the-century photograph captures the atmosphere and feel of the village at that time. Sir John Soane, who rebuilt the Bank of England, was born here. The Royal Oak, now a private house, can be seen at the top of the street.

WHITCHURCH, OLD TOLL GATE 1910 62230
The Whitchurch Tollbridge Company was established in the 18th century: a distinctive Victorian bridge of lattice ironwork spans the Thames between Whitchurch and Pangbourne, one of only two remaining toll bridges on the river. Pedestrians cross the bridge free of charge.

ABINGDON, MARKET PLACE 1890 26994
The imposing Jubilee statue of Queen Victoria dominates Abingdon's Market Place. Behind it is the striking facade of the Queen's Hotel, and on the left, by the entrance to the distinctive Corn Exchange, is a sign advertising excursions to Portsmouth.

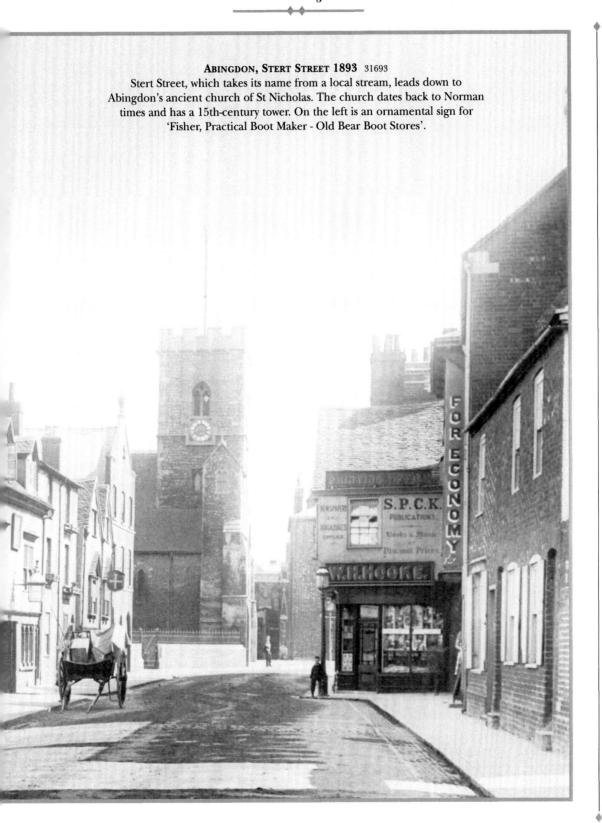

ABINGDON, STERT STREET 1893 31693
Stert Street, which takes its name from a local stream, leads down to
Abingdon's ancient church of St Nicholas. The church dates back to Norman
times and has a 15th-century tower. On the left is an ornamental sign for
'Fisher, Practical Boot Maker - Old Bear Boot Stores'.

ABINGDON, THE BOAT HOUSE 1890 26987

The punts and rowing boats have long since disappeared, and the Boat House has been demolished, though the landing stage is still used by Thames pleasure steamers from Oxford. The large house between the trees was built on the site where the Abbey Kitchener once lived.

ABINGDON, VIEW FROM THE ELMS 1890 26988x

A view of Abingdon and Nag's Head Island from the south bank of the Thames. On the left is the old County Gaol. The large building to the left of the cottages on the extreme right of the picture is the old Abingdon Carpet factory.

ABINGDON, THE LOCK FROM BELOW 1890 26990
The punts and rowing boats have long disappeared, replaced by narrow boats and motor cruisers. Long before the lock was built, an ancient channel known as Swift Ditch was probably the main navigation here.

ABINGDON, THE ABBEY MILL 1890 26992
The Abbey Mill was originally a corn and fulling mill. The unusual 13th-century gabled chimney of the Checker (or Exchequer) building can be seen behind the old stone cottages in Thames Street. The cottages were part of the south front of Abingdon Abbey and consisted of a granary, bakehouse and brewhouse.

CULHAM, THE COLLEGE 1900 45208
This photograph depicts Culham College, a neo-Gothic training school for schoolmasters founded by Bishop Wilberforce in 1853 to accommodate 130 students. The nearby village of Culham lies on a curve of the Thames, and is noted for its bridge built by Christ's Hospital and damaged during the Civil War.

SUTTON COURTENAY, THE VILLAGE 1890 27001
Once a royal manor, until Henry II gave it to the Courtenays, the village of Sutton Courtenay has several notable buildings. The 14th-century Abbey was built on land which once belonged to Abingdon Abbey, and was used as a summer retreat by the monks there.

DIDCOT BROADWAY C1955 D108055
Didcot is famous for being a major junction on the Western Region main line. The town has grown up around the junction, and today stands in the shadow of a huge coal-fired power station built in the 1960s.

NUNEHAM COURTENAY, AN OXFORD STEAMER 1890 26969
This stretch of the Thames is the setting for Nuneham Park, described by Horace Walpole as the most beautiful place in the world when he saw it in 1780. The classical mansion and village were built by Lord Harcourt, with parts of the grounds laid out by Capability Brown.

DORCHESTER, THE VILLAGE 1924 76211
The Romans built a town here, though its ramparts are now only faintly recognisable, and in Saxon times it was the bishopric for Wessex and Mercia. The abbey, at the heart of Dorchester, dates back to the 12th century. The White Hart Hotel and garage can be seen along the street.

CLIFTON HAMPDEN, THE VILLAGE AND THE CHURCH 1890 27006
Clifton Hampden includes an assortment of picturesque cottages and striking period houses. The church, located on a cliff overlooking the Thames and noted for its distinctive spire, was designed by Sir George Gilbert Scott, who was also responsible for the Albert Memorial and St Pancras Station in London.

CLIFTON HAMPDEN, FROM THE BRIDGE 1890 27008
The village church is seen here from the Gothic, six-arched river bridge of 1864, which links Clifton Hampden with the Barley Mow inn. The bridge was designed by Sir George Gilbert Scott: it is said that he sketched out the design on a shirt cuff. Locally-made coarse bricks were used to build it.

CLIFTON HAMPDEN, THE BARLEY MOW INN 1890 27010
The Barley Mow is one of the most famous and historic inns on the Thames. Jerome K Jerome featured the pub in 'Three Men in a Boat', published a year before this picture was taken. He described it as 'the quaintest, most old-world inn up the river'. The inn's thatched roof, low beams and oak panelling survive today.

Index

FRITH PRODUCTS & SERVICES

Francis Frith would doubtless be pleased to know that the pioneering publishing venture he started in 1860 still continues today. Over a hundred and forty years later, The Francis Frith Collection continues in the same innovative tradition and is now one of the foremost publishers of vintage photographs in the world. Some of the current activities include:

INTERIOR DECORATION

Today Frith's photographs can be seen framed and as giant wall murals in thousands of pubs, restaurants, hotels, banks, retail stores and other public buildings throughout the country. In every case they enhance the unique local atmosphere of the places they depict and provide reminders of gentler days in an increasingly busy and frenetic world.

PRODUCT PROMOTIONS

Frith products are used by many major companies to promote the sales of their own products or to reinforce their own history and heritage. Frith promotions have been used by Hovis bread, Courage beers, Scots Porage Oats, Colman's mustard, Cadbury's foods, Mellow Birds coffee, Dunhill pipe tobacco, Guinness, and Bulmer's Cider.

GENEALOGY AND FAMILY HISTORY

As the interest in family history and roots grows world-wide, more and more people are turning to Frith's photographs of Great Britain for images of the towns, villages and streets where their ancestors lived; and, of course, photographs of the churches and chapels where their ancestors were christened, married and buried are an essential part of every genealogy tree and family album.

FRITH PRODUCTS

All Frith photographs are available Framed or just as Mounted Prints and Posters (size 23 x 16 inches). These may be ordered from the address below. Other products available are - Address Books, Calendars, Jigsaws, Canvas Prints, Postcards and local and prestige books.

THE INTERNET

Already ninety thousand Frith photographs can be viewed and purchased on the internet through the Frith websites and a myriad of partner sites.

For more detailed information on Frith products, look at this site:
www.francisfrith.com

See the complete list of Frith Books at: www.francisfrith.com
This web site is regularly updated with the latest list of publications from The Francis Frith Collection. If you wish to buy books relating to another part of the country that your local bookshop does not stock, you may purchase on-line.

For further information, trade, or author enquiries please contact us at the address below:
The Francis Frith Collection, Unit 6, Oakley Business Park, Wylye Road, Dinton, Wiltshire SP3 5EU.
Tel: +44 (0)1722 716 376 Fax: +44 (0)1722 716 881 Email: sales@francisfrith.co.uk

See Frith products on the internet at www.francisfrith.com

FREE PRINT OF YOUR CHOICE
CHOOSE A PHOTOGRAPH FROM THIS BOOK
+ £3.50 POSTAGE

Mounted Print
Overall size 14 x 11 inches (355 x 280mm)

TO RECEIVE YOUR FREE PRINT

Choose any Frith photograph in this book

Simply complete the Voucher opposite and
return it with your remittance for £3.50 (to cover
postage and handling) and we will print the
photograph of your choice in SEPIA (size 11 x 8
inches) and supply it in a cream mount ready to
frame (overall size 14 x 11 inches).

Order additional Mounted Prints
at HALF PRICE - £12.00 each (normally £24.00)

If you would like to order more Frith prints
from this book, possibly as gifts for friends and
family, you can buy them at half price (with no
additional postage costs).

Have your Mounted Prints framed

For an extra £20.00 per print you can have your
mounted print(s) framed in an elegant polished
wood and gilt moulding, overall size
16 x 13 inches (no additional postage required).

IMPORTANT!

❶ Please note: aerial photographs and photographs
with a reference number starting with a "Z" are not Frith
photographs and cannot be supplied under this offer.

❷ Offer valid for delivery to one UK address only.

❸ These special prices are only available if you use this
form to order. You must use the ORIGINAL VOUCHER on
this page (no copies permitted). We can only despatch
to one UK address.

❹ This offer cannot be combined with any other offer.

As a customer your name & address will be stored by Frith but not sold or rented
to third parties. Your data will be used for the purpose of this promotion only.

Send completed Voucher form to:
**The Francis Frith Collection,
6 Oakley Business Park, Wylye Road,
Dinton, Wiltshire SP3 5EU**

Voucher for **FREE** and Reduced Price *Frith Prints*

*Please do not photocopy this voucher. Only the original is valid,
so please fill it in, cut it out and return it to us with your order.*

Picture ref no	Page no	Qty	Mounted @ £12.00	Framed + £20.00	Total Cost £
		1	Free of charge*	£	£
			£12.00	£	£
			£12.00	£	£
			£12.00	£	£
			£12.00	£	£
			£12.00	£	£

*Please allow 28 days
for delivery.
Offer available to one
UK address only*

* Post & handling		£3.80
Total Order Cost		£

Title of this book . . . .

I enclose a cheque/postal order for £ . . . .
made payable to 'The Francis Frith Collection'

OR please debit my Mastercard / Visa / Maestro card,
details below

Card Number:

Issue No (Maestro only):   Valid from (Maestro):

Card Security Number: Expires:

Signature:

Name Mr/Mrs/Ms . . . .

Address . . . .

. . . .

. . . .

. . . . Postcode . . . .

Daytime Tel No . . . .

Email . . . .

Valid to 31/12/15

Can you help us with information about any of the Frith photographs in this book?

We are gradually compiling an historical record for each of the photographs in the Frith archive. It is always fascinating to find out the names of the people shown in the pictures, as well as insights into the shops, buildings and other features depicted.

If you recognize anyone in the photographs in this book, or if you have information not already included in the author's caption, do let us know. We would love to hear from you, and will try to publish it in future books or articles.

An Invitation from The Francis Frith Collection to Share Your Memories

The 'Share Your Memories' feature of our website allows members of the public to add personal memories relating to the places featured in our photographs, or comment on others already added. Seeing a place from your past can rekindle forgotten or long held memories. Why not visit the website, find photographs of places you know well and add YOUR story for others to read and enjoy? We would love to hear from you!

www.francisfrith.com/memories

Our production team

Frith books are produced by a small dedicated team at offices near Salisbury. Most have worked with the Frith Collection for many years. All have in common one quality: they have a passion for the Frith Collection.

Frith Books and Gifts

We have a wide range of books and gifts available on our website utilising our photographic archive, many of which can be individually personalised.

www.francisfrith.com